CALLED TO HOLINESS

Bernard Häring, CSSR

CALLED TO HOLINESS

 St Paul Publications

ACKNOWLEDGEMENT

As for many of my previous publications, my heartfelt thanks to Mrs Josephine Ryan for her help in typing and final editing of this book as well as for her constructive suggestions about the content.

Bernard Häring, CSSR

St Paul Publications
Middlegreen, Slough SL3 6BT

Copyright © Bernard Häring, CSSR
Nihil obstat: M. J. Byrnes, ssp, stl
Imprimatur: F. Diamond, vg
First published in Great Britain, January 1982
Printed by the Society of St Paul, Slough
ISBN 0 85439 199 1

St Paul Publications is an activity of the priests and brothers of the Society of St Paul who promote the christian message through the mass media.

CONTENTS

Introduction	7
1. Lord, show us the way	12
2. Love is the answer	18
3. A grateful memory	26
4. Hope and trust	33
5. Lord, here I am	39
6. The gift of discernment	44
7. Grace and peace, peace and joy: God's gifts	48
8. In the school of the Crucified	53
9. Saints and sinners	59
10. In the communion of saints	65
11. Holiness is mission	70

INTRODUCTION

WRITING a book entitled, "Called to Holiness", I can envision to a considerable extent the mind of my readers. Only those who already have a desire to become holy — to be saints — will take time to read these pages; and my hope is that during the reading this already existing desire will increase. And what a splendid reward it would be for the author if, while dedicating his meditations, prayers and efforts to help a few people find the way to Christian holiness and stay on it to the end, he himself would also take a few steps forward with them!

But I have yet higher hopes, for I am not the only voice addressing you. Others have already planted the seed and watered the garden. God himself is totally interested in our quest and will not deny any grace to those who pray for it. Here, indeed, is something for which we can truly pray in the name of Jesus, for to be holy is our supreme vocation. We believe that the Holy Spirit, promised by Christ, is the Sanctifier, the great artist who forms saints, and that this is, for you, for me and for all humankind, the master-plan of the Father. Christ has ratified this master-plan by his life, death and resurrection. I am only one voice in a great choir that sings out the invitation of the Lord, "Become a truthful image of God".

On a hot summer day in 1963, I was working in a Council commission which drafted a text on the universal vocation to holiness and an appeal to those in religious life to be witnesses and promoters of this vocation which they should see as essential for their own identity. When, at noon, we left the room, we heard that Pope John XXIII was in the last agony. All of his life and his acceptance of death stood for the Council document on this universal vocation to holiness (Dogmatic Constitution on the Church, ch. v).

This text is at the very heart of the Council. Those who do not take it seriously enough will not understand anything about the teaching and guidelines of the Second Vatican Council or, indeed, of the Bible, which is God's word inviting us, most kindly and urgently, to "Be holy, for I, Yahweh, your God, am holy" (Lev 11:44; 19:2; 21:8).

We are, by grace and faith, God's offspring, born to a new life in Jesus Christ. Before God, his angels and saints and all his sons and daughters, the calling to holiness is the highest title of nobility. What a fool one is who refuses this noble title! If both liberals and traditionalists would first take this challenge to heart and translate the Council teaching into their own and their communities' life, we would come easily to agreement on most of the burning issues which seem so divisive today. The differing opinions on a thousand minor issues would not at all divide us any more.

It should be clear to all of us that assent to this doctrine does not make any sense unless we make it the central concern of our heart, mind and will. "How do I become holy?" is not just a question among many others; it is the greatest personal question of our lives. Of course, we do not dream of being among those whom the church canonises as outstanding saints and models. What matters is that we enrich the life of Christ's holy church and that, finally, God will find us faithful to this sublime vocation and his sanctifying action.

A lady, who had begun to realise how vital this question is, came breathlessly one day to a man who was praised by many as a saint, Francis de Sales, the author of the wonderful book, "Introduction to a Devout Life". She asked him, "How do I become holy?" His rather puzzling response was, "Would you, please, close the door more gently?" What the wise man meant by this advice came close, I think, to what a bishop said recently to an assembly of major superiors: "The first and most urgent service a bishop can offer to his diocese and a major superior to his communities is this: 'Be holy, right now!'" Holy in all things. Let holiness impregnate and mark your character and all of your conduct. St Francis de Sales had, by nature, a stormy character but made the words of the Lord, "Blessed are those of a gentle spirit" (Mt 5:5) the leitmotif of his striving for holiness. He experienced such a transformation that he was gentle toward all creatures and acted gently even in the way he closed doors, out of reverence for God and people. Perhaps his charism of discernment told him that this woman also needed such a leitmotif in her striving for holiness.

Ending this introdutcion, I want also to tell you and myself, "Be holy right now. Start, this moment, to seek holiness first!" In my case, age and illness make it particularly clear that any delay would be madness; but even if you are young and strong, nothing can justify delay. God wants you to be holy now. That means that you will renew wholeheartedly your fundamental option for fidelity to God's calling. You will respond with heart and mind and all your conduct, "Lord, here I am! Call me and guide me on the road to you!" And in the time to come, you will make your reading of the Bible, your participation in the liturgy, your meditation and your discernment about action all expressions of your burning desire to be holy *right now*. Never miss the next step possible that leads you in the right direction.

Dear Reader: At this point I invite you to take as basic reading, not only as parallel reading for this book but for your whole quest for holiness, the Sermon on the Mount (Mt chs 5 to 7) and the Farewell Discourse (Jn chs 13 to 17). If you do so, you will no longer be able to doubt or forget that the vocation to holiness is the central message of the Bible. You will also see much more clearly what it means.

* * *

God, our Father, from the beginning of our life you call us your children, and day by day you call us to become ever more aware of your wonderful design for us: to become a mirror-image of your goodness, kindness, generosity and wisdom. You leave no doubt that you have created and redeemed us for nothing less than a life that honours our status as your children, members of the family of the redeemed.

How could I ever forget such a sublime calling? You call us not just for some work to do but for BEING, for becoming your masterpiece. And we exist in full truth only if we accept your master-plan to make us holy, gracious, loving and lovable people.

Lord Jesus Christ, you called Peter, Andrew, John, James and many others to live in your company and thereby to recognise the model of a fulfilled life, the true image of the Father, the embodiment of holiness on earth. You instructed them kindly and patiently about the Father's design to make them holy. In the same way, you call me and so many millions of people, each individually by name and all of us together, to an intimate friendship with you. You came, not to make slaves but to make friends, and you invite and urge me to be one of them. There can be no hesitation on my part, for there is nothing more noble or attractive than this calling to be and to live as your friend, totally dedicated to the kingdom of your Father which you have proclaimed.

Come, Holy Spirit, enkindle my heart, my mind, my spirit, my will. Fill me with everlasting gratitude for this calling. I know quite well, and even from some painful experiences, that without your grace I can do nothing on the road to holiness. I cannot even grasp fully what it means. But you are the great promise of Jesus, the great gift of the Father and the Son. Breathe upon us, convert us, guide and guard us. Make us holy.

I pray not only for myself but for all the readers of this small book and, indeed, for all who promote the universal calling to holiness and all who yearn for a holy life. Nor do I forget those unfortunate people who care more for everything else than for the fulfilment of the Father's design, the Son's message, or for your promptings, O Spirit of God!

I pray that we all may follow this supreme vocation for our benefit and the benefit of all humanity.

Come forth, O Holy Spirit. Make us holy and renew the face of the earth.

1. LORD, SHOW US THE WAY!

" 'Set your troubled hearts at rest. Trust in God always; trust also in me. There are many dwelling-places in my Father's house; if it were not so I should have told you; for I am going there on purpose to prepare a place for you. And if I go and prepare a place for you, I shall come again and receive you to myself, so that where I am you may be also; and my way there is known to you.' Thomas said, 'Lord, we do not know where you are going, so how can we know the way?' Jesus replied, 'I am the way; I am the truth and I am life; no one comes to the Father except by me.'

" 'If you knew me you would know my Father too. From now on you do know him; you have seen him'. Philip said to him, 'Lord, show us the Father and we ask no more.' Jesus answered, 'Have I been all this time with you, Philip, and you still do not know me? Anyone who has seen me has seen the Father. Then how can you say, "Show us the Father"? Do you not believe that I am in the Father, and the Father in me? I am not myself the source of the words I speak to you; it is the Father who dwells in me doing his own work' " (Jn 14:1-11).

JESUS' farewell discourses (Jn 13-17) tell the enchanting story of his friendship with his disciples. He opens to them the depths of his heart and prepares them for the great event of the Paschal Mystery, the summit of redemption.

Here we receive a wonderfully clear vision of our calling to holiness as Christ's disciples, indeed as his friends and even sharers of his own life and love. He calls us to nothing less than holiness in an intimate union with himself, with his love for the Father and his love for all people.

Jesus' farewell is a promise to go to prepare a place

for his disciples. "There are many dwelling-places in my Father's house . . . I am going to prepare a place for you." The disciples whom Jesus called to follow him during his earthly life enjoyed his company and friendship. We, too, should know that he is now calling us to that same friendship, "so that where I am, you should be also; and my way there is known to you."

Thomas, who wants to see and touch everything concretely, listens intently. He is passionately eager to know the way of which Jesus speaks, with all its implications. But how can a person know the way if he does not even know where he is to go? "Thomas says, 'Lord, we do not know where you are going, so how can we know the way?' " And Jesus' answer is also the heart of the matter for us in our quest for holiness: what is the goal and the way to it? "Jesus replied, 'I am the way; I am the truth and I am life; no one comes to the Father except by me.' "

The goal of our life is the Father: to know him who has called us into being by knowing us in his love. Jesus comes from the Father, is sent by him to reveal to us his love, his truth, his life, and our own origin and end. The fruit of holiness is to know God blissfully as our loving Father, the Father of our Lord and brother, Jesus Christ, and finally to see him face to face. Jesus, having come from the Father, returns to him through his self-offering love and resurrection. But he does not want to return alone or only for his own purpose. He wants to bring all of us with him home to the Father as his holy people.

Jesus, the messenger of the Father, is not just one of the prophets; he is the "I-Am". He is one with the Father in his eternal divinity and one with him in love and glory. His humanity is taken up forever by the divine personhood of the eternal Word of the Father. He knows the way to the Father, for the Father is always with him, one with him in the power of the Holy Spirit, in mutual, self-giving love.

Yahweh, who revealed himself to Moses under the

names "I-Am" (Ex 3:14) assures Moses: "I am with you" (Ex 3:12). In Jesus Christ the "I-Am" reveals himself fully and finally as "God-with-us": *Emmanuel*.

The Father, Yahweh, has sent his Son — who, being one with him has also the name "I-Am" — to meet us where we are, in our misery and weakness. In Jesus, the Father waits for the prodigal son. Not only by word but by his whole being and his life and death, Jesus makes known to us the Father's compassionate love for his sons and daughters who left his house and were lost in sinfulness and alienation. "While he was still a long way off, his father saw him, and his heart went out to him. He ran to meet him, flung his arms around him and kissed him" (Lk 15:20).

The law-bound, correct older brother could not understand the father's action. He thought that his prodigal brother should first be disciplined and then treated according to his misdeeds. The prodigal himself did not imagine that more could be granted him than the status of serfdom.

By this parable, Jesus tells us plainly that those who turn to God with a sincere heart will receive from him a renewed calling to intimate friendship, to an on-going feast of grateful love. Wretched as we are and unable to reach God, we have no reason to despair or to doubt that we can become holy; for Jesus — the "I-Am" and the "I-am-with-you" — is running to meet us in our misery and weakness, running to embrace us and to walk with us all the way to the Father's house. He is the absolute pledge of the faithful God that we are called to holiness. He tells us plainly, "I am the *Way*", and commits himself to guide us on the road. And being on the road with us, he is already our "home", insofar as we really follow him and turn heart, mind and will to him.

The Father, who reveals himself in Jesus and is our final home, is the *Truth*. Jesus is both the Word in whom the Father speaks out all that he is, and the Word "breathing the Spirit" (Thomas Aquinas), "breathing love". Only this Spirit of Truth, the gift of the Father and the Son, can inscribe in our hearts the supreme truth that God is love.

Jesus is the liberating Truth. In the power of the Holy Spirit, he shows us the truth of his love and his total freedom for love by giving himself up for us on the cross. By everything that he is and does, he teaches us through the Holy Spirit that only loving people can know the Father and the Son. Thus he becomes the saving truth for all who respond faithfully to his calling.

In Jesus, the "I-Am", is our *Life*. He himself explains our life and vocation to holiness by the parable of the vine and the gardener. "I am the real vine, and my Father is the gardener . . . dwell in me, and I in you . . . If you dwell in me, and my words dwell in you, ask what you will and you shall have it. This is my Father's glory, that you may bear fruit in plenty and so be my disciples. As the Father has loved me, so I have loved you. Dwell in my love" (Jn 15: 1–9).

Jesus is so much our life that he shares with us his life-giving love relationship with the Father. Or we can equally say that the Father loves us so much that, through Jesus (who is our life) he shares with us the very love in which he eternally speaks his word and sends us his Incarnate Word, Jesus. Thus Jesus reveals to us the deepest meaning of our vocation to holiness. He takes us by the hand, identifies himself with us and asks us to let his own truth, the truth of Infinite love, shine in us and through us.

Like Philip, we are far from understanding the full wealth and bliss of the words, "I am the Way, I am the Truth, I am the Life"; but happy are we when, like Philip, we pray from the depths of our heart, "Lord, show us the Father and we ask no more" (Jn 14: 8).

If we pray for good health, success and other things, and also for holiness, we have missed the mark. We really begin to be true adorers of the one God and are on the road to holiness when we pray first and utmost for the purifying, liberating and saving knowledge of the Father: to "know the Father" in love and in a way ever more fruitful for salvific love. This prayer is all-inclusive. Then we can pray also for health and other things, but always in view of how these gifts may contribute to the knowledge of the Father, the True Love. In this way we are praying that God's will be done, for God himself wants us to have "plentiful salvation". "This is eternal life: to know thee who alone art truly God, and Jesus Christ whom thou hast sent" (Jn 17:3).

Praying for the supreme gift "to know the Father" is the same as praying, "Lord, make us holy". And if this is truly our one prayer, our one heart's desire, then we know that we are praying to the Father in the name of Jesus. We are opening ourselves to the very gift that Jesus and the Father most desire to grant us. And Jesus has assured us that "Indeed, anything you ask in my name I will do, so that the Father may be glorified in the Son" (Jn 14:13).

In this context, Jesus speaks a surprising word. "In very truth I tell you, he who has faith in me will do what I am doing; and he will do greater things still because I am going to the Father" (Jn 14:12). He speaks of a loving faith by which the disciples entrust themselves wholly to him and accept him gratefully as "the Way, the Truth, the Life".

Through faith we become one with Jesus and, like him, we are open to the promptings of the Father through the Spirit. More and more we become conformed with Jesus, who can say in its absolute sense, "It is the Father who dwells in me, doing his own work" (Jn 14:10).

Jesus prays to the Father for those who believe in him: "Consecrate them by the truth; thy word is truth. As thou hast sent me into the world, I send them into the world, and for their sake I now consecrate myself, that they too may be consecrated" (Jn 17:17–19). Consecrated in that truth which breathes love, we are sanctified; and this implies essentially a mission for the life of the world.

Sanctification, the vocation to holiness, is the greatest

gift, but a gift that allows no self-centredness. If we are holy, we are given to others and, like Jesus, we give ourselves to others. We receive and accept the others as a gift of the Father. This builds up a wholly new vision of all our relationships.

Jesus answered Philip: "Anyone who has seen me has seen the Father" (Jn 14:19). Those "see" Jesus truly who believe in him, turn their hearts, minds and wills to him, do everything to know him with heart and mind, and do his work in the world: the work of Love. It means they knowingly allow the Father to do his own work in them and through them, as he did with Jesus.

* * *

I thank you, Lord Jesus, eternal Word of the Father and radiance of his splendour, for having taken our flesh and spoken your wonderful message in human words. You made yourself the visible image of the Father. With all my heart I am longing to see you face-to-face in your glory. I am grateful, therefore, for the many ways you have already allowed us to know you through the marvels of your created universe. Seeing the beauty of the mountains and valleys, of flowers and animals, listening to the songs of the birds and of the winds, contemplating the countenance of holy people and knowing their goodness, compassion, generosity and purity, everything cries out to me: "Turn to him who made all this for you, revealing his own and his Father's beauty in all his words!"

Jesus, I thank you for the apt and graceful parables, symbols, images of the Bible, for everything that directs our attention to you.

In special hours of grace, it seems to me that your eyes rest on me and you invite me to "see" you, to "hear" you. Purify my heart and open my eyes and my ears. For only one thing matters now to me: to see you, to know you, and thus to see and to know the Father. Lord, show us the way. Teach us to know you who are the Way, the Truth, the Life.

"Lord, show us the Father and we ask no more!"

2. LOVE IS THE ANSWER

> "Love is patient; love is kind and envies no one. Love is never boastful, nor conceited, nor rude; never selfish, not quick to take offence. Love keeps no score of wrongs; does not gloat over other men's sins but delights in the truth.
>
> "There is nothing love cannot face; there is no limit to its faith, its hope, and its endurance.
>
> "Love will never come to an end . . . In a word, there are three things that last forever: faith, hope, and love; but the greatest of them all is love" (1 Cor 13:4–13).

SAINT Alphonsus wrote to his confreres: "To love him is the greatest work we can achieve on earth" (Letter of July 29, 1774). He knew it is the greatest work because it is the Father's own work. If we are to live on the level of children of God, brothers and sisters of Jesus, we should be, as Jesus was, ever conscious of "the Father who dwells in me doing his own work" (Jn 14:10).

Without God's grace we can do nothing on the level of salvation and sanctity. When I say "love is the answer", I have in mind especially two dimensions. The first is: what really matters is redeemed and redeeming love. Only in the light of the all-encompassing love of the Redeemer and the redeemed can we answer the question, "How can I become holy?" The second is: our love for God and neighbour has value and strength only as our answer to God's own love, for human holiness is unthinkable except as response to God's santifying action in the grace of the Holy Spirit.

We are attracted to holiness by divine grace and calling because God himself is gracious and attractive in his love. It is he who graces us, justifies us by grace through the gift of faith. That love which we call "the answer" and "the heart of the matter" in our quest for holiness does not originate in us. We are not its source. It is a central truth of salvation that God *first* loved us. We are loving and lovable only because he has created us to be sharers of his triune love and makes us a new creation by the Holy Spirit. He transforms sinners into saints by loving us and implanting in us the seed of his love.

Modern man is proud to be called an "achiever". There is a special "Who's Who" book to list the most successful achievers. But woe to us if we transfer this approach to the quest for holiness! Those who boast, "I did it! I made it!" are out of the running on the road to holiness.

Holy people are grateful and gracious receivers. They are thoroughly aware that reconciliation, sanctification, holiness, can be thought of only with the thankful praise, "From first to last this has been the work of God" (2 Cor 5:18). And this awareness dispels any tendency to idleness, delay or passivity. Whoever has grasped the truth that God first has loved us and now calls us to holiness in love by bestowing on us his own holy love and sanctifying us by his own truth, will hear Paul's words: "Sharing in God's work, we urge this appeal upon you: you have received the grace of God; do not let it go for nothing" (2 Cor 6:1).

To know Jesus and the Father is also to know the true countenance of love and the wonderful way God has loved us and loves us right now. Thus we learn the greatest art, the art of loving God.

St Alphonsus wrote a kind of moral theology for average people who desire to become holy. He titled it, "The Art of Loving Jesus Christ". It could as well have been, "How to Become Holy", for the two meanings are the same. When the saint was an old man, almost blind, a brother read to him from the book. Alphonsus exclaimed, "What a beautiful book!", not realising that it was his own.

Knowing that the art of loving Jesus Christ implies joining Jesus in his love for people, Alphonsus took as a basic text for his book the tender song about love in Paul's first letter to the Corinthians. Paul calls it "the best way" to holiness. "Now I will show you the best way of all" (1 Cor 12:31). "I may speak in tongues of men or of angels, but if I am without love, I am a sounding gong or a clanging cymbal. I may have the gift of prophecy, and know every hidden truth; I may have faith strong enough to move mountains; but if I have no love, I am nothing. I may dole out all I possess, or even give my body to be burnt, but if I have no love, I am none the better" (1 Cor 13:1–3).

Paul surely did not despise these wonderful charisms and qualities. What he means is that they have their real value and meaning as gifts of God's love, and can be received and administered truthfully only in that love which is the appropriate answer to God's own love.

In this song of praise, Paul gives a clear picture of what love really is. In Christ, God has revealed himself as the One who *is* Love. So where Paul says "love", we can say "Christ" or "the Father". Only thus can we understand the infinite dimensions of that love which "is patient, is kind and envies no one . . . is never boastful, nor conceited, nor rude; never selfish, not quick to take offence . . . keeps no score of wrongs; does not gloat over other men's sins but delights in the truth". There is indeed "nothing that (this) love cannot face" and "no limit to its faith, its hope and its endurance".

St Augustine said that "the singer himself is the new song". If we have become in Christ a new creation, gladly accepting our vocation to holiness, then we can not only sing with Christ the song of redeeming love but we ourselves can become a part of the song. The redeemed and redeeming love by which we follow Christ is the most beautiful melody in which heaven and earth, God and his saints, delight.

Christ leads this marvellous choir in which even the lame, the blind and the mute can have an active part. He sets the tone by his own patience and kindness. If, in difficult situations, we listen attentively to his clear voice and see his *patience* on the cross, his patience with us, his *kindness* to his imperfect disciples and even to great sinners, then our own song will blend ever more harmoniously in this great melody.

"*Love envies no one*". The voice of envy can never sing the new song. If we realise that we are new creatures in Christ and that "God's love has flooded our inmost heart through the Holy Spirit he has given us" (Rom 5:5), how can we dare to bring the disharmony of envy and anger into the song of the redeemed?

"*Love is never boastful*". Because Christ is ever aware that all he is and all he does comes from the Father, his whole life and death are a song of praise of the Father. For those who sing in the choir of Christ, the same should be true. If our love is a conscious response to God's own love, then we know that he alone is the "fountain of all holiness". Therefore, we do not boast; we give to God the honour that belongs to him.

And yet, and yet . . . In the charming little book, "Prayers from the Ark", we find a proud rooster who, perched on his dung-hill each morning, crows to the dawning sky, "Lord, I am your servant; but do not forget that it is I who make the sun rise!" We smile, of course, at this foolish bird, but do we not recognise him sometimes in our own desire to draw attention to ourselves instead of to God who is doing his work in us, and to the many people who have made our accomplishments possible?

If one is tempted to boast, to glorify oneself, I would like to suggest here the "paradoxical intention" recommended by a wise psychologist (Victor Frankl) as an amusing and effective antidote for taking oneself too seriously. Good humouredly, one simply declares aloud an exaggerated version of one's hidden intention: "Now I want to crow to the world about my brilliance, my skills (or my generosity, piety, remarkable insights, or whatever) instead of giving God and my friends the honour!" This self-knowing sense of humour quickly unmasks the temptation and tells the devil, with a smile, that we now know to whom the honour belongs and that we intend to render to God what belongs to him.

If we are fully conscious that our life is to be lived as part of Christ's great choir of the redeemed, then surely we will never be *"rude"*. Looking at Christ and hearing him, we shall develop a fine sensitivity against everything that is unfit in this company of singers who, in all their being and conduct, are also a part of the "new song".

"Never selfish". Selfishness is the antithesis of redemption. Whoever answers wholeheartedly the calling to holiness in Christ will sharpen sight and hearing to recognise all the enchanting lures of the old Adam. If we are fully engaged with Christ in the song of love, we shall quickly discover this enemy of the redeemed in all its disguises. One of its disguises is the constant and loud claim to personal rights, importance, even "justice". But we can easily unmask all these self-delusions if our eyes and hearts are ever open to the divine love that manifests itself as saving justice and mercy for all.

Love (Christ) *"is not quick to take offence"*. Christ prays even for those who crucify him, and dies for us who so often have offended him. He has come to seek the sinner, the offender.

"Keeps no score of wrongs". To keep score of wrongs pollutes our memory, disturbs our mind, and makes us unfit for the great song of love. Here again the "paradoxical intention" is a useful antidote. When wrongs done to us by others keep running through our mind like a nagging tape, disturbing our peace, we can smile before the mirror and tell our image that "my majesty is terribly offended; therefore I have a perfect right to take out my frustration on everyone around me!" But then we become more serious and speak to the Lord: "Lord, how great is your reign! How great were the offences you suffered from me and others, and how petty are these things that I am storing up in a resentful memory!" We can make

this thought tangible by stretching out our arms toward the vastness of God's kingdom, and then measuring with a tiny space between thumb and forefinger the relative size of our own complaint. But always we end with a prayer that the Lord may set us free, through the power of true love, from this hurtful habit of keeping score of wrongs.

In our community in Rome, I had an old friend who died at the age of 91. All the members of the community gave witness that they had never heard him speak of another's faults. Never to *"gloat over other men's sins"* is a tremendous achievement of love, but an achievement that is necessary for all who want to sing the new song of love in Christ's choir.

God's enemy, Satan, must feel flattered if even Christians tend to give prime attention to what is wrong with others. This gives Satan first place; he receives more attention than God. In truth, we can sing God's glory only if we always discover and acknowledge first whatever is right, good and beautiful. Thus we *"delight in the truth"* of love, whereby we help one another ever more creatively to discover the energies and beauties of that true love with which the Spirit fills our hearts.

"There is nothing love cannot face". Christ could face even the horrifying reality of his cross and all the insults that went with it. He faces Judas who betrays him with a kiss, and still calls him "friend", assuring him that even then he would still receive him back as friend if he would return to him in sincere conversion. He turns his merciful eyes to Peter who disowns him three times. Such love is the great victory of the cross, a victory that will forever shine in the risen Lord. If we are risen to a new life with him, we shall realise that love is the only right answer even to insults and calumnies. Then we can face illness and suffering, failure and frustration, and discover that, here and now, we can prove that our answer of love is sincere and strong.

Love lends its beauty, strength and depth to faith, hope and endurance. It abides forever. Christ, who came to earth to "sing the new song" tells us that love is the greatest, the all-encompassing reality, the most sublime beauty, the mightiest strength, the full truth and firm ground of our hope. And our hope is for a share in the everlasting feast of love.

To put love first in no way reduces other values. Rather, it opens the whole treasure of virtues and charisms. Paul exhorts us: "Put love first; but there are other gifts of the Spirit at which you should aim" (1 Cor 14:1). In this context, he exalts "*prophecy*". This is the clearsightedness of the loving person, the gift of discernment. Love recognises its true needs and expressions. We can never say, then, "Have love and do what your selfishness wants", for this is plain contradiction. But we can say with St Augustine: "Have love and do what this love bids you!" Christlike-love finds ever the right response. In it we will discover the appropriate answer even to complex situations.

* * *

We praise you, Father, Lord of heaven and earth, for having spoken the final and perfect Word of Love into our world. You have given us Christ to offer you, in our name also, the full answer of redeeming love. Let our life, as life in Jesus Christ, become the new song which will begin here on earth and come to its eternal consummation in heaven.

Instil in our hearts a great desire to know you and to know your Son and Messenger, Jesus Christ, to know your love and to know ever better how to respond in all events and times to your love and grace.

Lord Jesus Christ, your love has drawn me to you. The first taste of this love awakens in me hunger and thirst for an ever greater experience of this love and for the art of joining in your love of the Father and of all people. There are some who try to tell me that you do not want my love, since you do not need it. But whoever begins to know you realises that there is more than a need-love. Love is your being and your message; love is your invitation. It is the mystery of your heart and the revelation of your Father's love. A loving father and mother want to be loved because they are loving, and not because they have selfish needs. Much more is this the case with your love and your Father's love. You are love for each other in the power of the self-giving Spirit, and love for us. Your cry on the cross, "I am thirsty" is the thirst of a loving heart to see the beloved able and willing to love you and thus to come to their truth in your truth.

We praise you, Holy Spirit, and thank you for having poured out your love into our hearts. You are given to us by the Father and the Son to fill us with redeemed and redeeming love. Forgive us for so often seeking many other things first while giving second place to what you are and what your great gift is for us: love. Instil in our hearts the hunger and thirst for true love and the absolute trust that, with this love, all the other good things will come.

3. A GRATEFUL MEMORY

> "When the appointed time came he took his place at table, and the apostles with him; and he said to them, 'How I have longed to eat this Passover with you before my death! For I tell you, never again shall I eat it until the time when it finds its fulfilment in the kingdom of God'.
>
> "Then he took a cup, and after giving thanks he said, 'Take this and share it among yourselves; for I tell you, from this moment I shall drink from the fruit of the vine no more until the time when the kingdom of God comes'. And he took bread, gave thanks, and broke it; and he gave it to them, with the words: 'This is my body which is given up for you; do this as a memorial of me'" (Lk 22: 14–20).

OLD Jewish wisdom tells us in the Talmud that "ingratitude is even worse than theft". And, indeed, few thieves are more contemptible and ungracious than those who own many things and know thousands of "truths" but never acknowledge that they have received them from God and from the goodness and co-operation of countless people. It is hard to imagine anyone more deprived, more underdeveloped than the one who cannot give cordial thanks and cannot see the essential dimension of reality, that everything is the gift of a loving Father and destined for mutual gratitude. Lacking gratitude and a grateful memory, such people cannot share in the fruitfulness of history, since they neither recognise past generations nor discover the splendour of the present moment. They even disown their own basic truth, their self as gift, requesting gratitude. They steal the honour from God and deprive themselves of all the bliss.

The Venerable Sister Celeste Crostarosa, foundress of the Redemptoristine Order, saw the whole Christian life

— the road to holiness — as an insertion of oneself into the life and work of the Holy Redeemer through a "eucharistic memory", a grateful memory centred in the Eucharist. ("Eucharist" means literally "thanksgiving"). Here Christ, and through him the Father, assures us that he does not forget us. By his presence in the gift of himself and through the power of the Holy Spirit, we are reminded of all that Christ has done for us.

Essentially, the power of humankind and of each person and community to mould history depends on a healthy, grateful memory. A memory is healthy and faithful if it keeps alive all the wonderful deeds of God and all the good inheritances from past generations. It opens to us the treasures of the past, gives a sense of continuity, and illumines our present possibilities and responsibilities. It sees one's past in the light of salvation history, of the history of all of humankind, with Christ as centre. And it knows what to save and what to discard, thereby avoiding confusion.

The disciple of Christ has already a head start for an ordered memory. In a kind of marvellous symphony we bring into our daily celebration of the one Eucharist our life story, the life story of our family, our community, our parish and friends, our nation and the family of nations, the blessedness of the saints, the rescue of the sinners who found mercy. We render thanks to the Father for the work he has begun in us and carries on in order to make us his masterpiece, each one unique but all of us in the image of Christ and thus in his own image.

In a eucharistic memory we can remember and acknowledge our past sins in a healing way. As we praise God's mercy for his forgiveness, the very remembrance of our own sins heals hurt memories and moves us to mercy and generosity, making us ever more sharers in God's merciful faithfulness.

The gospel shows us Jesus as a great storyteller and as one who has lived the greatest story. By his story, retold by his disciples, he shapes the history of the church, of her saints, indeed, the history of humankind. We, too, are tellers of stories. But of what kind? Are our stories, true, rich, beautiful, constructive? Are they in praise of God's work and thus a part of our song of love? Or are they disagreeable recitations, hurtful, boastful, destructive? Are they chaotic or do they contribute to the master picture of salvation history? Are my stories a part of the "life in Christ Jesus"?

The eucharistic celebration constantly reminds us that "to render thanks always and everywhere is the way that leads us to salvation". For my part, since I believe that I truly can become holy if I remain faithful to this leitmotif of gratitude, I want to make this point as emphatic as possible.

A good start is to train one's memory by counting often, in meditation and prayer, God's blessings, his gracious gifts. (This can also be a blessed use of our few sleepless hours). We further train ourselves to see all events of our life and our times in the light of salvation history, of creation through the word of God and in view of the Incarnation of the Word of God, his life, passion, death and resurrection. We admire the beauty of creation and redemption. A tiny flower can remind us of the beauty of holy people or of all the beauty that God reveals to us. As for the remembrance of disturbing events, hurts, failures and frustrations, we bring them into the remembrance of Christ's passion and death.

When the doctor told me positively that my throat cancer made inevitable a tracheotomy and larynxectomy, there were some hidden tears but also a "dance before the Lord", surely not for the cancer but for the gift of faith which allows me to make sense of such situations and to bring them home into the Communion and thanksgiving with Christ. When the cancer again became active after a period of uncertainty, I felt, "Now, to render thanks always and on all occasion becomes the real thing". Yet since I am only a beginner, this song of a mute man does not flow as easily and strongly as I might wish. But when it enters into the eucharistic celebration where Christ gives himself and shares with us the power of his Spirit, then a grateful memory breaks through with its grace and strength.

It is easier for some people than for others to bring their heavy crosses into the Eucharist and see clearly that these crosses are not dead relics but a living share in the cross of Christ, and already touched by the power of the resurrection. There may still be temptation, however, to complain about smaller things. The memory may need more training, so that it will always quickly recall that the Eucharist, the "thanksgiving", is the key.

At a time when my vocal chords had already refused to sing but I did not yet dare to think it might be cancer, I lost my keys, including the key to the Jesuit house where I was a guest. I retraced my steps, insofar as I could remember them, but there was no sign of the keys. I went to bed somewhat worried, not only about the considerable nuisance of replacing all my own keys but even more about having lost my hosts' key. But early next morning, I woke from a dream that I had found the keys and was rendering thanks to God for having found them. Thus far it was only a dream. But under the impact of the thanksgiving which ended my dream, I went to one of the avenues of the city and there, in the recess of a pillar, I picked up the keys. Really. I was happy to have them, of course, but I also wondered if the experience might have a deeper meaning. Could it mean, perhaps, that to render thanks for all that the Lord sends us and asks from us is really the key?

A grateful memory is even the key to the key: to prayer. Mahatma Gandhi tells us that prayer is the key that closes our heart and house to the powers of darkness and opens us to the light. As long as our memory is not grateful, our prayer will be reduced to the recitation of our miseries, and we shall be in danger of looking at God from a "user's" point of view. But if gratitude is the fundamental note, we shall praise God even while we offer prayers of petition.

We praise him for allowing us to approach him, for inviting us to come to him with confidence, for reassuring us that he will give us even better things than we can ask for, if we pray in the name of Jesus. So we offer our prayers of petition with thanksgiving. We thank God beforehand for what he really intends to give us.

We praise him and thank him when we ask forgiveness for our sins, for he assures us even before we ask that he is a forgiving and healing Father. We praise him when we express our hopes, for he gave us his promises and reveals his faithfulness to us in so many ways. We thank him for everything, especially in trying situations.

Let us not miss the mark when we meet difficulties, contradiction, misunderstanding, calumnies, suffering. You may ask, "But how can I thank God at such a time? First, I cannot believe that God wants all this, and second, all my energies are spent in withstanding the evil, so how can I render thanks in the midst of it?"

To the first objection I can only call attention to Christ, who never ceased to praise the Father while accepting suffering and death. He thus transformed suffering into the most sublime test of trust in the Father and love for us sinners, in expiation for the sins of the world. We shall come back later to this important dimension on the road to holiness.

To the second objection I say that, in times of turmoil, we will be able to withstand the evil and heal whatever can be healed, only if we keep alive our grateful memory and energise it. In that way, our energies are not dissipated and wasted by impatience or anger, and our memory is not encumbered by negative impressions.

As practical advice I suggest that, for the first moment, we leave aside the thought of the trouble and gather all the most evident reasons for rendering thanks for so many gifts and benefits. Then we finally see the trouble in its proper proportions. In comparison with all the reasons for gratitude which we bring fully to consciousness by the act of praise and thanksgiving, it will appear small. In this way we regain our peace of mind and collect our energies to withstand what needs to be withstood, and in taking upon ourselves what cannot be avoided, changed or healed.

Our thanksgiving should continue until we feel that the Spirit takes up this task and fills us with a new understanding and a yet deeper gratitude. But again, let us remember that our leitmotif of gratitude implies that we bring all this into the Eucharist and activate a grateful memory of the passion, death and resurrection of Christ. Our thanks are offered in union with the eucharistic Christ!

One dimension of this key truth must be constantly kept in mind: that our thanksgiving offered to God is inseparable from gratitude to our neighbour. Unless we are grateful to people, our thanksgiving and eucharistic celebrations are disincarnate, unreal; they hang somewhere in a cloudy sky.

In a truthful eucharistic memory there is also full acceptance of oneself: "It is good for me *to be*, since all that I am and all my capacities are God's gifts". And those with whom we live and make our life's journey should be able to sense also our basic feeling and deep conviction: "It is good that *you* are!"

If we live by the truth that the others are a great gift of God for us, we will spontaneously and frequently see the many reasons to be grateful to them, and will speak out this feeling. Gradually we will also come to a new understanding of the service others justly request from us. Indeed, they do us a service if their real needs prompt us to make the right use of our own God-given faculties.

Of course, we cannot deny that people sometimes become burdensome to us, and that misunderstandings and unjustified antagonisms do hurt. But if we faithfully use the master-key of gratitude in all situations, then we gradually realise that even in some unpleasant ways people have helped us to come closer to God and to learn a more truthful, Christlike love.

Making thanksgiving and a grateful memory one's master-key or leitmotif has its impact on all of life, personal, social, economic, national, international. How many friendships and marriages could be saved and become precious if people would stop reviving unhealthy memories and recall, instead, the many good things they have shared? How many political compromises would result in more justice for all if each party would remember the good contributions of the other? Our history books, too, should recall the good deeds and contributions of other nations, especially those with whom our nation is sometimes in conflict.

Does not the whole world need a refreshing turn to gratitude as leitmotif: gratitude to God and to the countless people who, out of their own gratitude for his gifts, have contributed to the good things we have today?

* * *

I thank you, Father, for allowing me to join your beloved Son, Jesus Christ, in his sacrifice of praise. I praise you for accepting my poor act of thanksgiving and teaching me the deepest dimensions and the highest beauty of thanksgiving, through the Eucharist. And for the experience that a grateful memory is the road and key to peace and strength, I also thank you.

Send forth your Spirit to pray in us, to purify our memory and our intentions, and to lead us into a life of thanksgiving and praise. Let all our brothers and sisters discover this key or find it again if they have lost it.

Lord Jesus, I thank you for the Eucharist in which you invite us to join you in constant praise and thanksgiving, where you assure us that you never forget us, and where the church keeps alive her memory of all that you have done for her and for all of humankind. I thank you for reminding us in the Eucharist that "rendering thanks always and on all occasions" is the master-key to salvation and holiness.

Forgive me, Lord, for so often distorting my memory, for encumbering it with ceaseless repetition of unpleasant and resentful memories. I thank you not only for having forgiven me but also for gradually healing my memory and teaching me how to use the key of a grateful memory.

4. HOPE AND TRUST

> "And why be anxious about clothes? Consider how the lilies grow in the fields; they do not work, they do not spin; and yet, I tell you, even Solomon in all his splendour was not attired like one of these. But if that is how God clothes the grass in the fields, which is there today, and tomorrow is thrown on the stove, will he not all the more clothe you? How little faith you have! No, do not ask anxiously, 'What are we to eat? What are we to drink? What shall we wear?' All these are things for the heathen to run after, not for you, for your heavenly Father knows that you need them all.
>
> "Set your mind on God's kingdom and his justice before everything else, and all the rest will come to you as well. So do not be anxious about tomorrow; tomorrow will look after itself. Each day has troubles enough of its own" (Mt 6:27–34).

TO BECOME holy is an enterprise too great for human forces alone. Only if we remember that this is God's initiative, God's calling and will, shall we never lose heart. By putting all our trust in him, and constantly praising him in gratitude for this precious gift, we shall be able to persevere.

The basis of our hope and trust is God's faithfulness. But our big question is whether our response will be faithful unto our death. More and more we realise how far our own fidelity lags behind God's own faithfulness to his people.

The liturgical prayers of Israel are marked by this realisation, and give us the key. By her ongoing praise of Yahweh's fidelity and mercy, Israel opened herself repeatedly to the restoring action of God. This is also the way of the church. She knows that her achievements and her fidelity are nothing to boast of; but she knows, and manifests beautifully in her liturgy, that in the praise of God's faithfulness and mercy she experiences God's power to renew and strengthen her. She is consoled and encouraged by her saints who, in this paean of thanks and praise, have given a faithful response. Even great sinners have thus found the road to faithfulness. And this will happen time and again.

Sometimes when I heard confessions of people who, after a long period of grave sinfulness were truly repentant, I assured them that they would have all the divine promises if they tried honestly to please the Lord in all things — if, in other words, they would start on the road to holiness; but that we have no divine assurance whatsoever if we want no more than mediocrity or external correctness.

Of course, we all have to remind ourselves rather frequently about this consoling and challenging truth. As long as we are striving sincerely for nothing less than one hundred percent dedication to God's kingdom, this truth is consoling, strengthening and comforting. But as soon as we look for a kind of bargain in the service of God, it becomes a fearful truth, for we would be depriving ourselves of God's promises given for those who accept fully their being called to holiness.

Decades ago I saw advertisements for tithing which presented the idea as "ten percent for God, ninety percent for yourself". I cannot easily imagine a more dangerous slogan. If I am "tithing" ten percent of my money, time, energy and attention to God while reserving ninety percent for my selfish self, I am indeed an idolater, making myself, in my thinking and conduct, nine times more important than God. But then, of course, the God to whom I give ten percent is no longer the living, all-holy God.

The true meaning of the Old Testament tithing was to give ten percent for the cult, the priests and the poor, thus reminding oneself that all that we are and all that we have are God's gifts and must be used in a way that honours the giver of all good gifts. If, in addition, we put aside ten percent of our time for the sacrifice of praise and for meditation, then this makes sense if our intention is to become better able to honour God in all the rest of our time and activity.

What miserable "tithing" it is if a Christian avoids certain sins only out of fear of hell: if he aims no higher than to keep out of hell! He may look in all the sacred writings but he will find not one word of God that gives divine assurance that such people really will not go to hell. If anyone wants to stop sinning only where mortal sin begins, by necessity that person will miss the mark and fall into the abyss.

We respond faithfully to the divine promises and commandments if, with all our heart, we desire to become holy, and seek here and now the appropriate next step in that direction. We honour God if we expect great things from him, and he himself offers us the greatest thing: to become holy.

Hope and trust in God tell me that I can overcome my laziness, my faint-heartedness, my selfishness and everything that could block me on the road to holiness.

God does not give empty words as promises. Behind the words stand his faithfulness and his *deeds*. And we should see all his wonderful works and deeds in the light of the sacraments which are, at the same time *sacraments of faith* and *sacraments of hope*.

In *baptism* God justifies and sanctifies us, graces us and calls us his beloved children. Cyril of Jerusalem used to tell the neophytes of his time that the Father, who from heaven said to Jesus, "Thou art my beloved Son", was now telling them, "You have become my children". If the almighty God accepts us as his sons and daughters, together with Jesus Christ, how could he then forsake us?

In the sacrament of *confirmation*, he anoints us by the power and joy of the Holy Spirit and assures us that he wants us to become his mature sons and daughters. This sacrament is a firmer promise than all the oaths of men. God, who has begun the work, will complete it if only we respond with trust and hope, and strive honestly to be faithful.

The *Eucharist* not only gives us the master-key, the all-embracing thankfulness, but also is the nearness and power of the Holy One, the assurance that Jesus is present not only externally but wants to continue, in us and for us and indeed for the whole world his work of redemption and sanctification.

Old oriental eucharistic liturgies are particularly enlightening for our vocation to holiness. A eucharistic litany lets the faithful respond to all petitions with the synthesising prayer, "Lord, make us holy; Lord, make us one!" Christ, who has told us so clearly that he wants us to be one with him and one among us all, as the vine and branches are one, teaches us that holiness is, above all, the vital expression of our oneness in him and with him.

In the same liturgy before communion, the deacon warns and invites all the faithful in a loud voice: "The Holy One for the holy!" This would be a frightening admonition in a static concept, for who would dare to say, "I am already holy"? But the real meaning is that the recipients of Holy Communion should ask themselves, "Do I sincerely intend to respond faithfully to the vocation to holiness?" It is not so much a question of whether we have sinned gravely in the past, but rather, "Am I truly sorry for all my sins, and do I still intend, in spite of all my weakness, to trust that God really calls me to holiness?" So each time we receive Communion, we should explicitly renew and deepen our purpose to become holy and to look for the next possible step that brings us closer to God.

If, through mortal sin, a Christian has turned away from God (has reversed his own fundamental option for the kingdom of God to an option against God's love and holiness), then according to Catholic doctrine, he has to receive the *sacrament of reconciliation* (if possible) before receiving Communion. There is no legalism in this commandment. It is a necessary requirement, since the Lord offers us this sacrament as a way of conversion and peace. The penitent then can receive Communion truly reconciled and as a sacrament of further purification and sanctification.

But the sacrament of reconciliation is not only for the "dead". Normally for us, it is a sacrament for the "sick" and weak. In this sacrament we go to the divine Healer before mortal sin can overcome us. Each reception of this sacrament is a conscious recognition that the way to full union with Christ (holiness) requires a radical purification.

If we understand the relevance of hope and trust in God in our quest for holiness, we will also gratefully allow him to destroy all our false hopes and our trust in our own forces and achievements, in material goods, and undisturbed health. The reasonable earthly hopes are good, but only if they consciously give first place to the hope for growth in the love of God, an active role in the kingdom of God, and the full and final union with God.

It is a good and necessary hope to look for personal salvation, for perseverance and holiness. It is Christian hope, however, only if we ardently hope for all these for our fellow travellers also, and help one another on the road. By essence, Christian hope is solidaric. But it is absurd to think that our hope for eternal life is truly an expression of solidarity if we are not ready to share the earthly goods with those in need. The picture which Christ gives us of the last and final judgement (Mt 25: 31–46) tells us how much our hope for holiness and for eternal life depends on how we use God's gifts for the needs of other people, especially of those who cannot reward us.

In this solidaric Christian hope, we look to the saints in heaven. Their lives encourage us: "if others could be so faithful to their vocation, why not I?" Our veneration of the saints and our prayer to them are expressions of the "communion of saints". They are authentic expressions, however, only if we are, at the same time, expressing our solidarity with our brethren on earth.

While we say that hope and trust in God allows and requires a certain distrust of our own forces, this is not the full truth. If we trust thoroughly in God, we can enjoy also a healthy trust in our own inner resources, since they are gifts of God. And at the same time we discover joyously the good in others, and help them to discover ever more their own inner strengths. The elements of distrust are thus healthily subordinated to the over-all climate of trust in God and of mutual trust.

* * *

Lord God, we praise you for the many signs of your faithfulness, for all you have done for us throughout the history of salvation. We praise you for the great sign of hope: the cross and death of your Son, the glory of his resurrection, the mission of the Holy Spirit, and the foundation of the church whom you have never abandoned despite her turmoils and weaknesses.

We thank you for the communion of saints and the many people around us who, time and again, have encouraged us.

Lord, teach us to praise you always for your faithfulness. And grant us the grace to pray faithfully and perseveringly. Grant us endurance and trust during life's troubles. And help us to become signs of hope and encouragement for many others.

O Mary, Mother of mercy, next to Jesus Christ the Father has given you to us poor sinners as a great sign of hope and trust. You know best the costly price your Son Jesus has paid for our salvation and for our sublime vocation to become an image of God's own goodness and sign of Christ's compassionate love for us all. Pray for us, that we may put all our trust in Christ and ask for nothing less than to become truly holy.

5. LORD, HERE I AM

> "At his coming into the world, he says: 'Sacrifice and offering thou didst not desire, but thou hast prepared a body for me. Whole-offerings and sin-offerings thou didst not delight in. Then I said, "Here am I: as it is written of me in the scroll, I have come, O God, to do thy will." '.
>
> "First he says, 'Sacrifices and offerings, whole-offerings and sin-offerings, thou didst not desire nor delight in' — although the Law prescribes them — and then he says, 'I have come to do thy will'. He thus annuls the former to establish the latter. And it is by the will of God that we have been consecrated, through the offering of the body of Jesus Christ once and for all" (Heb 10:5-10).

THE wealth of the present moment depends on the treasures of the past, made present by a grateful memory, and on the energy of our hope which decides the direction and provides the power of action and endurance. The past can bear fruit and the hope can be attained only through vigilance for the present opportunities and readiness to use them. This is the appeal of the Apostle to the redeemed: "Use the present opportunity to the full" (Eph 5:16). Those who do not "try to understand what the will of the Lord is" (Eph 5:17) here and now, miss the mark completely.

Right here and now, we have no other possibility to manifest our gratitude for all past events and our hope for the future than by a faithful use of the present moment. Andreas Dryphius expresses this beautifully:

> "None of the years are mine that time took away from me,
> Nor is the future mine that lies ahead of me.
> This very instant is my property;
> Be He in it who made time and eternity."

There is no better way to honour God's presence with us than to cherish the present moment with all its chances and even all its hardships.

One of the great enemies of our vocation to holiness is escapism into wishful thinking. The "if only" syndrome wastes our spiritual energies as much as complaining and discontent. Our vocation is to be holy here and now, and can be responded to only by the basic prayer of the saints, "Lord, here I am, call me; Lord, here I am, send me!"

Those who are gifted and graced by a grateful memory and by clearsighted hope have the best chance to discover what the present moment offers. Our expectation of the Lord at the end of history and at the end of our life is truthful only if we are watching for his coming and his call right now. The more we are ready to respond gratefully, the more alert will be our vigilance for the opportunities.

The most graced and holy among women, Mary the mother of Christ, expresses her readiness with the words, "Here I am; I am the Lord's servant" (Lk 1:38).

"Yes, Father, here am I" is an apt leitmotif for those who have made the fundamental option to follow the calling to holiness. Thus each moment confirms it and deepens its roots in our inmost being and in our life history.

We do not really live in the presence of the living God, the Lord of history, if we only remember that he is there. His presence is dynamic, active, creative, and if we live on that level, we shall be listening to his calling, attentive to his coming, and completely ready to respond to him faithfully and prudently, here and now. When our whole being spells out, "Here I am, call me!", we have the best chance to discover what pleases God.

Being vigilant and ready for God's coming and calling means also to be ever alert to our neighbour's needs and just expectations. Over and again we see in our own lives examples of how our neighbours, by their characteristics, needs and deeds, alert us to signs of God's grace and calling.

If those around us are kind, friendly and helpful, they provide an environment that invites us to render thanks to God, the source of all goodness, and to remember that, through the goodness of these people, he calls us to grow in his image and likeness, according to Jesus' word: "Let your goodness have no limits, just as the goodness of the Father knows no limits" (Mt 5:48).

If those close to us in life or at work are unhappy, unfriendly, or even hostile, then let us remember the Lord's word: "Be merciful as your heavenly Father" (Lk 6:36). He calls us to show compassion right now, and to help the other to overcome his unhappy mood.

If someone misinterprets our good intentions and blames us unjustly, then we remember that the Lord has forgiven us a thousand times and now comes to test whether we are truly trying to become ever more an image of him who lets his sun shine on the just and unjust.

If we pray, "Lord, here I am", when a person, through his needs, disturbs our plans and our comfort, we shall discover how far we can and must allow the other to impose on us and ask our help.

If anyone around us has the bad habit of telling what is wrong with other people, then our readiness to "be holy right now" will help us to discover how to let that person know that we see the good in him and also in the person whose faults he is reporting. We will consider which will help most: silence, with a kind of absent-mindedness while the tales continue, a pleasant reminder of something good about the victim, a smooth change of subject, or other device.

If we have been forgetful and are now discomforted by double work on that account, then we can learn to be patient with ourselves and to accept with a smile our common "human condition". Or we can apologise quietly to those whom our forgetfulness disturbed and try to train our memory better. What matters is that we do not waste the present moment in useless regrets, frustration or impatience.

And if we have once missed the mark by not readily responding to the present opportunity and God's grace, then let us trust that the Lord forgives us and calls us to ask forgiveness. And while doing so, we should not lose our serenity, for we need all our energies and peace of mind in order to use better the next moment.

I know a lady who has lost several of her children through tragic accidents and experienced many other hardships. When I tried to console her in these events, she said, "I have accepted this and do not complain; but now I must prepare myself for the next test to come". This woman was an outstanding example of what readiness is. Because she had prepared herself to live her life as it came to her, with loving attention to the needs of others, she was not tempted to yield to bitterness or self-pity. Like Job, she had a grateful memory and a no less great trust in God.

Many people block their readiness and discernment, and exhaust their best energies through useless regrets. These are the "if only" people who constantly dream that their lives could and would be happier and more fruitful "if only" their circumstances, their spouses, their children or friends, their environment were different. Many marriages break down because one of the spouses thinks and even says, "if only I had married someone else . . ." But if they had married that "someone else", the cry would still be the same if they had not freed themselves from this "if only" evasion. Another widespread habit is to lament the "bad times" while missing almost all the opportunities to work for better times.

* * *

Lord Jesus, you told us that man does not live by bread alone but by every word that comes from the mouth of God. And it was, indeed, your "bread" to do at all times the will of God. At each moment of your life you were vigilant and ready to please the Father by serving the poor, healing the sick, forgiving offenders, seeking those who had gone astray. Each moment was important to you, for you saw it in the light of the great hour in which you would say your final "Yes, Father, here am I!"

Help me to learn from you and from your beloved mother a similar vigilance and readiness. Help me to see, through all the veils, your coming, and to discover you under whatever disguise you call me. Make me ready for the great hours of my life, and vigilant for the thousand small opportunities to meet the needs of my neighbour by the best use of your gifts.

Let me understand ever better than I cannot pray sincerely, "Lord, here I am; call me!" unless I am attentive and sensitive to my brothers and sisters.

6. THE GIFT OF DISCERNMENT

> "Let no one deceive you by shallow arguments; it is for all these things that God's dreadful judgement is coming upon his rebel subjects. Have no part or lot with them. For though you were once all darkness, now as Christians you are light. Live like persons who are at home in daylight, for where light is, there all goodness springs up, all justice and truth. Try to find out what would please the Lord; take no part in the barren deeds of darkness, but show them up for what they are. The things they do in secret it would be shameful even to mention. But everything, when once the light has shown it up, is illumined, and everything thus illumined is all light. And so the hymn says: 'Awake, sleeper, rise from the dead, and Christ will shine upon you'.
>
> "Be most careful then how you conduct yourselves: like sensible people, not like simpletons. Use the present opportunity to the full, for these are evil days. So do not be fools, but try to understand what the will of the Lord is . . . Let the Holy Spirit fill you: speak to one another in psalms, hymns and songs; sing and make music in your hearts to the Lord; and in the name of our Lord Jesus Christ give thanks every day for everything to our God and Father" (Eph 5:6–20).

IF we confess "we believe in the Holy Spirit", this has much to do with our faith and with our trust that we are called to holiness. The Holy Spirit sanctifies us, guides us, converts us. From him come the indispensable gifts of wisdom and discernment. The more faithfully we adore the Holy Spirit and give thanks for all his gifts, the more he opens our hearts and minds for "discernment of the spirits", so that we may know whom we can follow and what cause we can support.

The gift of discernment has to do with means: what

next step is to be taken here and now, what people to associate with, and what approach to take. Discernment can work only if we have wholeheartedly decided on the right goal: to be holy, to strive always towards greater holiness, to seek in all things first the kingdom of God, and to allow the Holy Spirit to make us loving, discerning persons.

The chief task of discernment is to recognise the countenance of true love, a love in the image of God and the model of the Holy Redeemer. We can never become discerning persons guided by the Spirit unless our main purpose is to be, above all, loving, selfless, generous people. If our love were already wholly transformed into Christlike love, we would find spontaneously the best possible expression of this love. But since we are only on the road and still have to conquer our own selfishness and be aware of the many counterfeits of love in the world around us, we need clear and specific criteria.

Above all, we have to watch over our *motives*: are we truly seeking first the kingdom of God, the common good, healthy relationships with our neighbours? Or do we sometimes allow our self-importance, our ambition, or our resentment against certain people to influence our evaluation of situations and actions? People who give first attention to career tend to assess their actions mainly or only in terms of what serves this ambition. They will do a lot of "good", but only in view of their career. Therefore, many of their good deeds and words will be falsified, and they will be completely blind to many opportunities to do good.

Besides, good motives alone do not suffice; we need also *objective criteria*. But first of all we need to know the true countenance of love as described, for instance, in Paul's great song on love in 1 Corinthians 13. The commandments, their interpretation through the moral teaching of the church, and the doctrine on the virtues give us criteria for the appropriate articulation of love. But if one has no love or is not enough concerned about love, these criteria will not work when love demands a costly price, for their purpose is to serve true love under all circumstances.

Especially in conflict situations we realise that we cannot make the appropriate decision without a clear scale of values. Some people seem to be generous. They spend time and money and renounce personal advantage; but because they have not a clear scale of values and needs, they neglect the higher and more urgent needs of others and of the community, and may even block the best causes. The discerning person will never betray spiritual values in favour of material success or progress, never foster and promote economic and political goals to the detriment of peace and social justice on any level.

The discerning person takes seriously his or her various responsibilities for the common good, for the family, the church and state, for peace and social justice, for one's own and others' health. Hence, before we act we must consider carefully the foreseeable consequences of our intended actions and words. And if, in some cases, we lack knowledge and experience about the consequences, we shall take advice from more experienced and knowledgeable people.

The saints were ever eager to find a good spiritual adviser, but while seeking guidance they never betrayed their own conscience. Guidance does not absolve us from our personal responsibility but should enable us to act more responsibly and with greater competence.

Distraction and superficiality are common enemies of discernment. People who are truly discerning take time for meditation, for quiet moments before the Lord, for daily examination of conscience, and for careful planning of specific actions and encounters. They discern what is the most urgent task for them at this time and examine themselves regularly about particular purposes and projects. It is good to give account to one's spiritual guide.

The Spirit, who works in all, through all and for all, directs our attention to the discerning community. The principle of collegiality on all levels of the church expresses this striving for discerning communities. In a healthy family, important decisions are taken only after a serious dialogue in which everyone appreciates the contribution of the others.

To round up the picture on discernment, I want to recall here what has already been said: before each decision we should bring fully to life our grateful memory. And if we doubt our intention or decision, let us ask ourselves simply before the Lord: "Can I offer this or that sincerely to the Lord as an expression of my gratitude?" And if our conscience says "No", we reject the temptation.

St Nicholas Flue made his act of discernment in the light of his daily prayer, "Lord, grant everything that helps me on the way to thee; Lord, take away from me everything that hinders me on the way to thee". With such a prayer, one would surely look most carefully at all one's words and deeds, testing whether they faithfully carry out this intention.

Frequent self-examination in the light of the Our Father and the beatitudes of the Sermon on the Mount will help us to become ever more discerning persons.

* * *

Come, Holy Spirit, convert us, sanctify us, guide us, enlighten us, purify our hearts and minds so that we may be able to discern what pleases you. Free us from distraction and superficiality. Broaden our horizons so that we may be concerned as much for the good of others as for ourselves. Help us to see the needs of others in the light of your gifts to us. Make us vigilant and clearsighted for the present opportunities, and ready to use them generously and wisely.

Enlighten those who are guides in church and society, and let us discern well the signs of the times, seeing the many chances for growth even in the midst of alarming signs. Without you we are but fools and tend to lend others to folly. Hence we pray with all our heart: "Grant us the gifts of wisdom and prudence".

7. GRACE AND PEACE, PEACE AND JOY: GOD'S GIFTS

> "The Lord is near; have no anxiety, but in everything make your requests known to God in prayer and petition with thanksgiving. Then the peace of God, which is beyond our utmost understanding, will keep guard over your understanding, will keep guard over your hearts and your thoughts, in Christ Jesus" (Phil 4:6–8).

> "Peace is my parting gift to you, my own peace, such as the world cannot give. Set your troubled hearts at rest, and banish your fears" (Jn 14:27).

SAINT Paul, in words directed to all Christians, describes the road to holiness: "You are no longer under law but under the grace of God" (Rom 6:14).

There are two quite different classes of Christians. One is made up of those who ask constantly "Must I do this? Does law oblige me to do or to avoid this or that?" The other class, the true Christians who happily and gratefully accept their calling to holiness, ask quite differently "What can I render to the Lord for all his goodness? How can I best use the grace of God in response to the present opportunities?" These become ever more graced persons, gracious, grateful, generous and peaceful.

Paul greets the early communities with the words, "Grace and peace to you from God, our Father, and the Lord Jesus Christ" (Rom 1:7; 1 Cor 1:3; 2 Cor 1:2). Peace is Jesus' farewell gift before his passion, and again the greeting and abundant gift of the risen Lord. When his disciples heard his greeting, "Peace be with you", and they saw him, "they were filled with joy" (Jn 20:20). In the Bible, grace and peace, peace and joy go hand-in-hand.

When God turns his countenance to us and shines upon us, this is grace; and if, as graced persons, we are totally given to thanksgiving and praise, then our hearts are filled with peace and joy. We are light through divine light and can radiate this peace and joy to those around us.

For Master Eckehart and his disciple Blessed Henry Seuse, the key word was *Gelassenheit*, and all their prayer and ascetical endeavour centred around this precious gift of God. It means the profound peace of the soul from which flows serenity and a kind of imperturbability: a graced and trustful imperturbability, totally different from the *atharaxia* of the stoic ethics which despised the human passions and looked more for one's own quietude than for others' needs.

The peace and serenity of which we speak, following the great Dominican mystics of the thirteenth century, are the overflow of a tender and passionate love of Christ crucified and risen for us. And emanating from this is a heightened capacity to love people in Christ, to rejoice in all the wonderful works of God, and to minister with special care to the troubled.

Creative detachment is emphasised in view of the highest goal: total surrender to God. Blessed Henry Seuse defines *Gelassenheit* as "the peace and serenity of those who have found their home in God, so that they no longer know their own self in itself, but know all things and themselves in their origin". The disciple of Christ, who has found his peace in his Master, is no longer obsessed by the thought of what he needs but thinks rather of what he can renounce for the sake of Christ and his neighbour. The highest level of this peace and serenity is total, trustful surrender to God even in the hours of seeming forsakenness.

Yet there are few of us whose peace is not sometimes threatened and serenity diminished by disappointment, unjust treatment or other mishap. In those moments we can turn our minds to the tremendous disproportion between the greatness of God's love for us and the relative smallness of what disturbs us. Then we may sigh, "Lord, when shall I finally have totally entrusted myself to you and found all my peace and joy in you?"

Disciples of Christ know that they cannot train for peace and serenity by self-styled mortifications; neither have they an unhealthy liking for adversities. But when these are sent or allowed by divine providence, true disciples greet them as precious occasions for that creative detachment from self-centredness which helps them to find their centre wholly in God.

Grace and peace do not make Christ's disciples less sensitive to offences and misunderstandings, but allow them to see everything in the light of the crucified love of Christ and in proportion and relation to the kingdom of God.

Peace and joy set free all the human energies for seeking, discerning and doing God's will, and especially for commitment to justice and peace. Christ's disciples will not be surprised if, in this endeavour, they have to suffer and find contradiction. And knowing that authentic peace and joy are totally God's gifts, they realise also that they can neither preserve nor foster them unless they constantly give the honour to God.

In this sense St Paul writes: "Praise be to the God and Father of our Lord Jesus Christ, merciful Father, the God whose consolation never fails us! He comforts us in our troubles, so that we in turn may be able to comfort others in any trouble of theirs and to share with them the consolation we ourselves receive from God. As Christ's cup of suffering overflows, and we suffer with him, so also through Christ our consolation overflows" (2 Cor 1:3-6).

The peace of Christ is an indivisible gift and mission. It is a sharing in Christ's own life and peace that transforms our whole self and our whole life. "The peace of God which surpasses all understanding will keep guard over your hearts and thoughts, in Christ Jesus" (Phil 4:7).

We give special importance to this inner peace and

joy, not by a kind of pious egoism, not by lack of interest in others or in the welfare of church and society, but rather by total dedication to God's kingdom in all its dimensions, and especially to the cause of peace on earth. This makes us guard our hearts and thoughts, for we cannot share and radiate the peace and joy of Christ unless we appreciate and preserve them in heart and mind.

On the other hand, the disciples of Christ do not consider their peace mission as a threat to their own inner peace. They know, of course, that peacemakers have to pay the price of peace, just as Christ did; but they look even more at the power of the risen Lord. In their dedication, while they suffer on their Mount Calvary, they do not lose sight of the Mount of the Beatitudes and the promise of Christ: "How blest are the peacemakers; God shall call them his children" (Mt 5:9).

As far as we ourselves are concerned, we try to live with all people in peace and use only peaceful means in our mission, in accordance with the biblical injunction, "Do not let evil conquer you but use good to defeat evil" (Rom 12:20). The gospel of peace to which we are dedicated is, first of all, a challenge to root out in ourselves whatever causes unnecessary discord. But with the grace of God constantly implored, we can accept that sharp contradiction which so often is the reaction to an integral Christian life. We shall speak the truth in love, even where truth will lay bare the secret thoughts of unjust and violent people. While doing so, we shall not forget to speak out also, by words and conduct, the important truth that there is hope for everyone. Nobody is a hopeless case; all can convert to the liberating truth of love and justice. But it is only when our own hearts are filled with the peace of Christ that we can appeal effectively to the hearts of others, including those who oppose us.

Even our own weaknesses and the necessity to fight against our own faults should not jeopardise our inner peace or our capacity to radiate its joy, for we know that God is patient and will help us in our ongoing purification. Trust in redemption and in the faithfulness of the merciful God allows us to smile in spite of all our errors and limitations.

This gift, to smile despite our troubles and errors, shows a healthy sense of humour. It never hurts others; rather, it associates us with the weaknesses common to humankind and disallows any feeling of superiority. Thus, "speaking the truth in love" is not looking down on others. The sense of humour is a ray of sunshine arising from the hearts of people who are at peace in Christ. It can also appeal to those whose ideas, aims or outright injustices we sometimes have to oppose.

* * *

Father, we praise you because in Christ you chose us to be without blemish in your sight, to be full of love and peace, to be peacemakers, and thus accepted as your beloved children. Grant that the glory of your precious gift, so graciously bestowed on us in your beloved Son, may redound in peace and joy to the praise of your name.

Fill our hearts with your grace, so that we can live and proclaim the gospel of your peace by our whole being and conduct. Give us strength and wisdom to detach ourselves from all forms of slavery, from anguish, aggressiveness and useless worries, so that we may be totally free for your gospel of peace and joy.

Make us strong in the hours of temptation and dryness. Let us ever more experience how necessary and good it is to entrust ourselves wholly to your will. Help us to praise you in all events, especially in the hours of discomfort and failure, so that we may give space to your consolation, and thereby become ever more able to comfort others and to call them to the way of peace.

8. IN THE SCHOOL OF THE CRUCIFIED

> "And what of ourselves? With all these witnesses to faith around us like a cloud, we must throw off all encumbrance, every clinging to sin, and run with resolution the race for which we are entered, our eyes fixed on Jesus, on whom faith depends from start to finish: Jesus who, in place of the joy that was open to him, endured the cross, making light of the disgrace, and has taken his seat at the right hand of the throne of God.
>
> "Think of him who submitted to such opposition from sinners; that will help you not to lose heart and grow faint. In your struggle against sin, you have not yet resisted to the point of shedding your blood. You have forgotten the text of Scripture which addresses you as sons and daughters and appeals to you in these words: 'My son, do not think lightly of the Lord's discipline nor lose heart when he corrects you; for the Lord disciplines those whom he loves; he lays the rod on every son whom he acknowledges.' You must endure it as healing discipline: God is treating you as his children" (Heb 12:1–7).

TO DREAM of holiness without the school of suffering is tantamount to heresy and a great danger for salvation. Christ invites us to holiness and at the same time calls us to take upon ourselves our cross day by day, and thus to follow him. "If anyone wishes to be a follower of mine, he must leave the selfish self behind; day after day he must take up his cross and come with me" (Lk 9:23).

Christ's suffering unto death is the source of our reconciliation, salvation and sanctification. The cross, for him and for his disciples, is the way to resurrection. Our sacramental conformation with Christ writes into our innermost being the discipleship of the Crucified.

This does not mean that we should have a longing for suffering but that we should realise that the great commandment of love and saving solidarity cannot be carried to fulfilment without sharing in Christ's suffering. There are frustrations in our unavoidable struggle against our own selfishness, laziness and pride. There are our own and our fellow travellers' burdens which, for each of us, would be unbearable if we would not "bear the burden of each other and thus fulfil the law of Christ" (Gal 6:2).

Good psychology tells parents and other educators that they commit a deadly fault if they think that children should be spared all kinds of frustrations. While we have no right to radiate frustration or arbitrarily to put frustrations in their way, every child and adolescent, as well as ourselves, must come to realise that no one can grow to maturity without facing life's inevitable frustrations, especially in the indispensable fight against one's own selfishness. Parents, who know by their own experience how harmful it would have been if they had been allowed to yield to all kinds of selfish desires, must also know that it is a serious mistake and a sin against charity and justice to try to fulfil their children's unreasonable desires in order to avoid frustrations.

The epistle to the Hebrews teaches us in plain language about suffering in God's salvation plan. "It was clearly fitting that God, for whom and through whom all things exist, should, in bringing many sons to glory, make the leader who delivers them perfect through suffering" (Heb 2:10).

The all-merciful and compassionate Father reveals the depth of his love through his Son who shares with us the same flesh and blood, "so that through death he might liberate those who, through fear of death, had all their lifetime been in servitude" (Heb 2:14ff.).

Because of the reign of sin, humankind was exposed to destructive suffering. Jesus came "to expiate the sins of the people" (Heb 2:17), thereby transforming the meaning and purpose of suffering. Suffering and death bring Jesus closest to us and fill us with trust in the merciful God. "For ours is not a high priest unable to sympathise with our weaknesses, but one who, because of the likeness to us, has been tested every way, only without sin" (Heb 4:15). Jesus himself says: "There is no greater love than this, that a man should lay down his life for his friends" (Jn 15:13). The summit of this love is that the Son of God, made man for us, calls us who are sinners his "friends", although it was for our sins that he suffered so cruelly.

It was most appropriate that John Paul II called the man who shot him, "my brother". To do so in the midst of suffering and risk of death is something quite different from fine humanistic talk about brotherhood by people who are not touched by the misery of sinful humankind, and who do little to alleviate the burden of others, including even those who oppose them.

About Jesus, our leader and high priest, the epistle to the Hebrews dares to say: "Son through he was, he learned obedience in the school of suffering" (Heb 5:8). From beginning to end the obedience of Christ to the will of the Father was perfect, unlimited. From the perspective of human experience it is something different to say, "Thy will be done" when everything is going well than when one is faced with the gravest suffering. Jesus not only knows, by divine wisdom and human virtue, what surrender to the will of God is. He knows it also in the deepest dimension by surendering himself totally to the Father when he had been betrayed, delivered to the unbelievers and crucified like a common criminal.

For us, the learning process in the school of suffering has additional functions: expiation for our sins, purification from our selfishness, exercise of our strength to love and trust, and it offers us precious opportunities to learn compassion for others.

One of the strongest motives for accepting the school of suffering even gratefully — though not with "delight"

— is the configuration with Christ and the fruitfulness of suffering with him for the salvation of humankind.

We are easily tempted to think that we already enjoy the full and imperturbable peace of Christ when things are going well. Then, when a number of adversities, misgivings, misunderstandings and sufferings break over us, we realise how fragile that peace still was, and that its roots were not yet deep enough in us.

When, in the midst of a storm of troubles, Blessed Henry Seuse complained, the Lord asked him kindly, "Where now is your peace (*Gelassenheit*)?" Jesus taught his friend that peace comes to its fullness and depth only when the surrender of our will to the Father is tested in times of storm. But those who have a burning desire for full union with God and gradually understand the purifying function of suffering will be able "always and everywhere" to render thanks.

For some Christians, suffering becomes unbearable because they look at their own and others' suffering mainly as divine punishment. They have a fear of God which is a slavish fear, and this is depressing, for suffering cannot then have its liberating results. Our sins do cause punishment; they destroy our peace and joy. But if we have faith in the divine Redeemer and trust in God our Father, then we realise that God himself is not inflicting punishment but comes, rather, to reconcile and heal us.

Though we are sinners, we should turn to God with total trust in times of suffering. He wants it to be remedial, a step forward in salvation and sanctity. We should even hope that by accepting the suffering we can participate in the work of redemption "in Christ". Liberation from slavish fear is of tremendous importance in time of illness and suffering, even from a viewpoint of physical and psychic healing, but much more from the viewpoint of our vocation to holiness.

An old priest, when he read that Fathing Häring had throat cancer, publicised his "knowledge" that "God has punished him". When I read this letter in a weekly publication, I felt great compassion for this priest, for if he immediately thinks of punishment in the case of another's suffering, he will be tortured by the thought of divine punishment when suffering comes to him.

I doubt that I could have survived all the illnesses and difficulties of my life if I had looked on them in a perspective of "punishment". Of course, we all sometimes suffer because of our own faults, but even this does not mean that God "punishes" us. Rather, we can see that God kindly offers us an opportunity to learn by the consequences of our mistakes, and even more, to accept these consequences as a precious school of suffering in union with Christ who suffered for us all.

If we learn from Holy Scripture, then we know quite well that there are illnesses and sufferings not so much in view of "punishment" as in view of the opportunity to glorify God in union with Christ. Even great sinners can, through the gift of faith and grace, come to accept their sufferings as something precious. For instance, I remember (without applying the term "great sinner") a priest who, decades ago, left the priesthood and lived long years in an invalid marriage. He told me his painful experiences of inner and outer sufferings: of never having found an appropriate job, of his wife's permanent illness, the grave burden of his several children when he too fell ill, the drug addiction of one of his sons, and other troubles. The conclusion this man drew was "But I should give thanks to God after all, for I am afraid that I would have continued to be a domineering and proud priest. So God, despite all my faults, has taught me to be humble and not to judge anyone else".

* * *

Lord Jesus, how happy we are that you have loved us and will love us unto death! In union with you, we praise the Father for having sent you to take upon yourself our burden and to transform the meaning of suffering and death.

Lord, after all the experiences, I am still afraid of suffering, of illness and contradiction. I surely do not have to pray that you send me more suffering. Preserve me from suffering that goes beyond my powers; give me strength to accept whatever is my normal share in your sufferings and in the price of discipleship.

Let your Holy Spirit come upon us so that we can understand the meaning and healing power of our suffering, and bear it patiently in union with you and out of love for our brothers and sisters.

Grant us, O Lord, wisdom and generosity so that, individually and together, we may alleviate the suffering of our fellowmen and prevent unjust suffering.

9. SAINTS AND SINNERS

> "Here is the message we heard from him and pass to you: that God is light, and in him there is no darkness at all. If we claim to be sharing in his life while we walk in the dark, our words and our lives are a lie; but if we walk in the light as he himself is in the light, then we share together a common life, and we are being cleansed from every sin by the blood of Jesus his Son.
>
> "If we claim to be sinless, we are self-deceived and strangers to the truth. If we confess our sins, he is just and may be trusted to forgive our sins and cleanse us from every kind of wrong; but if we say we have committed no sin, we make him out to be a liar, and then his word has no place in us.
>
> "My children, in writing thus to you my purpose is that you should not commit sin. But should anyone commit a sin, we have one to plead our cause with the Father, Jesus Christ, and he is just" (1 Jn 1:5–2:1).

ALL Christians would substantially agree that they are neither simply saints nor simply sinners. But, for our question on how to become holy, it makes a great difference whether we say "sinners and saints" or, rather, "saints and sinners".

Looking at God's design and action, we surely must choose the sequence, "saints and sinners", for God has created us to be a mirror image of his own goodness, "to be without blemish in his sight". But if we look at ourselves from our own limited and self-centred vision, then we have to say "sinners". St Thomas says rightly that man is the first cause only of sin; in all that is good, the first source is God alone.

If we consider the time process of justification, then we realise that a person who is justified by grace after a sinful life should remember that he or she was not at all a saint but only a sinner before becoming a saint by God's action. Hence, we give praise for God's powerful grace and mercy.

Paul, who always remembers what a dreadful sinner he was, reminds the Christians that God justifies all of us by mere grace. "In our self-centred condition we, like the rest, lay under the dreadful judgement of God. But God, rich in mercy, for the great love he bore us, brought us to life with Christ even when we were dead in our sins ... For it is by his grace you are saved, through trusting him; it is not your own doing. It is God's gift, not a reward for work done. There is nothing for anyone to boast of" (Eph 2 : 3–30).

However, if we look at a Christian, a believer who accepts gratefully his vocation to holiness, the sequence "sinner and saint" would be quite a wrong emhpasis and a great injustice to God's justifying and sanctifying action. In spite of all our weakness and the dire need to fight the "old Adam" in us, the basic reality is that we are "saints". In the perspective of God's gracious action and wonderful design, the truth that we are sanctified and do happily accept our vocation stands high in comparison with our weakness and the work still to be done in us. It is good news and a strong incentive to strive for holiness when Paul tells us: "Thus you no longer are aliens in a foreign land but fellow-citizens with God's people, members of God's household" (Eph 2 : 19).

In his letters, Paul addresses the Christians simply as "saints": "I send greetings to all of you whom God loves and has called to be his holy people" (Rom 1 : 7); "to the church of God which is at Corinth, to those sanctified in Christ Jesus, called to be saints" (1 Cor 1 : 2; 2 Cor 1 : 1; Eph 1 : 1; Phil 1 : 1); "to the saints and faithful brethren at Colossae" (Col 1 : 1).

Paul and all great pastors and Christian educators after him have taken special care to make their fellow Christians gratefully aware that the basic truth about themselves is that they have been sanctified, although not in a way that would allow them to boast about themselves or become self-satisfied. On the contrary, the praise of God's sanctifying action and the sense of the nobility of being Christians provide the strongest motive for a holy life: "to worship him with a holy worship, with uprightness of heart" (Lk 1:74).

In the sight of God the fundamental truth about us is: "You have been through the purifying waters: you have been made holy and just through the name of the Lord Jesus Christ and the Spirit of God" (1 Cor 6:11). This makes it imperative to put to death our selfish self with its misdeeds. Sin has no right over us. We *can* live a holy life, we *want to* live a holy life and, of course, we *must* live a holy life. "Now you must yield your bodies to the service of righteousness, making for a holy life" (Rom 6:22).

A christian whose chief consciousness is of his own misery and sinfulness does injustice to God's gracious action. Such a person will be easily discouraged and not sufficiently motivated for a holy life. He may even tend to justify his sins somehow in a dangerous kind of "sin-mystification", saying: "We are all sinners; we cannot but sin and yet hope in God's mercy". But Christians who really see the sanctifying action of God as the prime reality will not excuse their sins. They know that the sins of those whom God has sanctified are, indeed, sinful in the light of the divine calling and grace.

Theology traditionally distinguishes between first justification and conversion, and second justification and the corresponding ongoing conversion and purification. The basic fact of justification and sanctification spells out clearly: "Let this become the full truth of your thoughts and your conduct; be more fully converted!"

The basic conversion to God and the corresponding justification and sanctifying grace go hand-in-hand with the Christian's fundamental option for a holy life, for God's reign within him and in the world. But then this fundamental option needs to be fully ratified, strengthened, embodied in attitudes, virtues and in all of our conduct.

Knowing that we are chosen and reconciled by God's graciousness and sanctified by the Holy Spirit, we can accept ourselves. We can be reconciled with our shades and thereby with our urgent need for further purification and constant striving for a holy life, never discouraged nor lazy, never self-satisfied, but also never despairing or faint-hearted.

When I insist that attention must always be given first to what God has done in us and to what he calls us, this by no means belittles our still threatening sinfulness (selfishness, pride, greed . . .). Rather, we see how sinful it is to yield to the desires of the "old Adam" or "old Eve". But knowing ourselves now wholly in the sight of the divine Redeemer and Good Shepherd, we can face truthfully and with a certain serenity the task of ongoing conversion.

Facing our shades and the threatening features of our selfish self in the light of God's action, and praising him always for his healing mercy, we also learn to accept others with their particular shades, and to be for them signs of God's healing action. We learn a deep reverence for others, with no exception.

St Augustine, who never forget what a sinner he was, warns us not to despise sinners, for some who are great sinners may one day be holier than we are. This profound reverence and this trust in God's power will help our neighbour, too, to discover his own inner resources coming from God.

The consciousness that we are, indeed, sinners as well as saints will make us more peaceful, more ready for dialogue and for constructive proposals. This applies also to conduct between nations. If we give prime attention to the evil in others and in ourselves, this will only make for cynicism and obstruct all efforts to build a healthier community and a healthier world. In the past, an arrogant self-righteousness has often led to most cruel "holy" wars that were wars of extermination.

Only those who believe in the universal vocation to holiness and, therefore, everywhere discover first the good on which to build will be able to offer fraternal correction with a gentle and encouraging attitude.

And if we are to face our task of ongoing purification with courage and realism, we shall have to distinguish carefully between detestable sinfulness and those shades which have little or nothing to do with selfishness and guilt. We should be equally cautious about following those psychoanalysts who try to explain everything by early childhood constellations or by external circumstances and those undiscerning "moralists" whose heavy judgements ascribe everything to people's bad will. We have to know that there are limits to our free will. We cannot, for instance, change all the negative traits of our heritage and character at once. Often a long time is required before we become really clearsighted. And even people who have reached a high level of holiness can still have some blind spots or be unable to overcome an ingrained habit.

On the other hand, we do injustice to God, ourselves and our mission to the world if we think that we cannot overcome mediocrity. If once we have come to the faith conviction that God really wants us to be holy, and we continue on the right path each day, our energies will grow steadily. Day by day we shall have a more sensitive conscience, and new horizons of goodness and generosity will emerge as we gradually discover the strength of the freedom of the children of God.

When we begin to feel the peace and joy arising from a deep union with God and full docility to the grace of the Holy Spirit, we also can face more courageously the demands of further purification. And while we go through the fire of this purification, the sense of union with Christ, the joy in his friendship, will stimulate us ever more.

* * *

We praise you Father, for in Christ you have chosen us before the world was founded, to be holy, without blemish in your sight, and full of love. You destined us — such was your will and pleasure — to be accepted as your children through Jesus Christ, so that the glory of your gracious gift, so graciously bestowed on us in your Beloved, might redound to your praise. For in Christ our redemption is secured and our sins are forgiven through the shedding of his blood. Therein lies the richness of your free grace lavished upon us, imparting wisdom and insight.

O God, let your Holy Spirit come upon us so that our life may manifest always our wonder and gratitude for what you have done for us and in us. Help us, so that all our life may praise you for your gifts. Make us living signs and witnesses of your design to call all men and women to holiness.

Open our hearts and minds so that we may be able to face, in the light of your gracious action, our still existing inclination to sinfulness, to be more thoroughly converted, and to live more truthfully according to the grace you have bestowed on us.

Help us, O Spirit of God, to discover the holiness in the people whom we meet, so that we may become better able to face the evil in the world and to combat the darkness in the world around us.

10. IN THE COMMUNION OF SAINTS

> "I entreat you for the Lord's sake: as God called you, live up to your calling. Be humble always and gentle, and patient too. Be forbearing with one another and charitable. Spare no effort to make fast with bonds of peace the unity which the Spirit gives. There is one body and one Spirit, as there is also one hope held out in God's call to you; one Lord, one faith, one baptism; one God and Father of all, who is over all and through all and in all.
>
> "But each of us has been given his gifts, his due portion of Christ's bounty. And these were his gifts: some to be apostles, some prophets, some evangelists, some pastors and teachers, to equip God's people for work in his service, to the building up of the body of Christ. So shall we all at last attain to the unity inherent in our faith and our knowledge of the Son of God — to maturity, measured by nothing less than the full stature of Christ" (Eph 4:1–13).

WE believe in the communion of saints: that we are a part of God's household, that the saints in heaven and on earth care for us, that we belong to them and they belong to us, and that they have a burning desire to see us walking on the road to holiness. Blessed are we if this faith determines all our thinking and striving; we shall be a blessing for humanity.

Whether we become holy or not is not our private business, our private gain or terrible loss. It matters for the whole world, for all of humanity. "Christ is like a single body with its many limbs and organs which, many as they are, together make up one body . . . God has combined the various parts, so that there might be no sense of division in the body, but that all its organs might feel the same concern for one another. If one organ suffers, they all suffer together. If one flourishes, they all rejoice together" (1 Cor 12:12–26).

To accept our vocation to holiness implies that we look carefully for what might be our special place in God's household. "In what profession and state of life can I best serve church and society? What kind of charisms has God given me, and how can I best use them to meet the most urgent needs of our brothers and sisters?" For me as for many others, these considerations provided the strongest motives for choosing the priestly vocation. My parents made an equally wise choice when they chose married life as their vocation, deciding together to found a family and to make their home a house of prayer, of goodness, of trust in God, and to raise children in full awareness of their Christian dignity and responsibility.

The church needs each one of us in our respective place. She is a holy church by divine calling and grace; but her shining in holiness depends on you and me, on all the members of the church. Her inner life and the fulfilment of her mission depend on the harmonious and effective interplay of all. Our mutual love and concern, our concord, are basic expressions of our belief in one holy catholic church, in the communion of saints not only in heaven but also on earth.

The church is given to us to proclaim the gospel, to ensure us the sacraments and to show us the road to holiness. We who need the church owe our allegiance to her, just as the church owes us her co-operation. Since the church is Christ's own foundation, our love for her and our fidelity to her are expressions of our gratitude to him.

The weaknesses and imperfections of the church can be no reason for not loving her or not listening to her. Jesus chose Peter to be the head of the apostles and loved him in spite of all his faults. John, the beloved disciple who faithfully stood under the cross and to whom the Lord could entrust his mother, had also shown some regrettable traits. He and his brother, the "sons of thunder", had wanted to call down fire on the village of the Samaritans who had refused them hospitality. And once they coveted the most distinguished places in Christ's kingdom, which they still conceived in the pattern of earthly power. But Christ's friendship and patient teaching finally bore the best fruits. In the hour of trial, John did better than Peter; and on the road to the empty grave — indeed, to the Easter faith — he was outrunning Peter, but then waited at the tomb so that Peter could be the first to enter it. He gave Peter love and honour, and thus encouraged him to run the race.

There can be conflicts among men and women in the church on important subjects, just as there were between Peter and the all-too-conservative community of Jerusalem (Acts, ch. 10). Paul even opposed Peter to his face "because he was clearly in the wrong" (Gal 2:9), but this did not at all mean rebellion or a lack of respect and allegiance.

It is unreasonable to leave the church or to stop loving her if one thinks that bishops have made a wrong decision. We ourselves have made false assessments many times and have failed in many ways, but this does not allow the church to stop loving us or to care less for us.

Leaving the church or looking down on her implies a considerable measure of false self-confidence and a great lack of gratitude to Christ, who loves the church so much and loves us too, with all our shades. To leave the church in protest means that one leaves behind St Francis of Assisi and all the others of the choir of saints who were faithful to the church on earth and now pray for her in heaven. It means separating oneself from Mother Teresa of Calcutta and so many other wonderful people of today's church. It means leaving even Mary, the mother of Jesus and of the church.

If we love the church with Christ's love, we care especially for Christian unity, for Christ's great desire and testament to his disciples is "that all may be one".

Veneration of the saints — those canonised by the church and those known only to God and the heavenly hosts — is an important part of the praise for God's marvels. If anyone tells us that, for the sake of God's own honour, he would not venerate the saints, we should ask him if he can honour a great artist by refusing to give attention to his masterpieces.

If the veneration of saints and angels is authentic, then it will not lessen but rather will deepen and strengthen our readiness to listen to the living saints, including the uncomfortable prophets and the most humble people.

The attentive reading of good biographies of saints is an important incentive and encouragement on the road to holiness. We gain new enthusiasm by seeing the diversity of life conditions and charisms, of character and leitmotif, and yet the marvellous harmony of those many voices in the choir of Christ. We also may discern what might be the most appropriate leitmotif for ourselves.

We praise God, above all, for having given us Mary, the mother of Jesus and our mother, as model of faith and holiness. From her we learn to make of our life a magnificat, one song of praise of God. She teaches us that God loves the humble ones, those who gladly serve others, and deciphers the signs of history as conflict between the humble and the arrogant. She tells us that we should have great hunger and thirst for holiness, and leads us under Jesus' cross and into the cenacle to pray with the church and for the church. She is pure crystal, her beauty reflecting the marvels of God. She turns all our attention to her Son and thus to the Father in heaven. And since she is the most noble member of the church, she teaches us how to love the church and to fulfil her expectation that we may bring joy and honour to her by becoming holy.

Each of the saints of the past and the present manifests particular charisms which show us how to respond to various needs in the diversity of situations. The lives of the saints tell us about humble beginnings, dire conflicts and astonishing developments. There are saints who seem to remain in hidden corners of the world, yet have enriched or do enrich the lives of many. There are others who for a long time seemed to live unimportant lives or at least were not able to offer the world outstanding examples, yet when God has required a great decision or has put a heavy burden on them, they have outgrown mediocrity and emerged as heroic examples of holiness.

A thoughtful look at the various saints — those who have died and those who live with us — gives us an idea of how blessed the world might be, how wonderful the interplay of social classes and nations, if at least those who claim to be believers would muster all their energies and, with willing hearts, set out to follow God's grace and calling. There is no one who is unable to add a new dimension of goodness, kindness, fidelity, creative liberty to the history of the world.

* * *

Lord God, by calling us to nothing less than holiness, you reveal to us your great love and our belonging to your family of saints. We thank you for the example and the prayers of the saints. We thank you for the holy church who leads us to you. Open our eyes to the treasures which the church on earth offers, and to genuine holiness even outside the visible church. Strengthen our trust in you through a better understanding of the solidarity of salvation of all the saints in heaven and on earth. They are a pledge of your goodness to us and your power to make us holy.

Help us to recognise ever more clearly the gifts you have given to each of us and to make the best use of them to the benefit of the church and of all people. Show us how we can best bear each other's burdens and thus help one another to reach the goal of our vocation to be holy.

Lord, make us holy! Make us one!

11. HOLINESS IS MISSION

> "You are salt to the world. And if salt becomes tasteless, how is it to be salted to be restored? It is now good for nothing but to be thrown away and trodden underfoot.
>
> "You are light to the world. A town that stands on a hill cannot be hidden. When a lamp is lit, it is not put under the meal-tub, but on the lampstand, where it gives light to everyone in the house. And you, like the lamp, must shed light among your fellows, so that, when they see the good you do, they may give praise to your Father in heaven" (Mt 5:13–16).

AFTER Christ and with Christ, the saints are the greatest benefactors of humankind. They receive and accept from God the great gift of holiness for the good of the whole world.

Christ himself says of his consecration that it implies mission: being "sent into the world" (Jn 5:36). And in his high-priestly prayer he says of his disciples, "As thou has sent me into the world, I have sent them into the world, and for their sake I consecrate myself, that they too may be consecrated by the truth" (Jn 17:17-19).

If we all were saints in faithful response to God's grace and calling, the world would be much more human, more at peace. The structures of economy and politics would be healthier and, above all, the world would experience the greatest riches, the wealth of redeemed and redeeming love and saving justice.

Each Christian is meant to be a source of sanctification for those closest to him or her. The very fact that God gives a person a holy Christian spouse is a sign that he wants to sanctify that person also. Paul writes: "The unbelieving husband is consecrated through his wife, and the unbelieving wife is consecrated through her husband"; and their children too "are holy" (1 Cor 7:14).

This means that if the Christian partner or parent follows his or her own vocation to holiness, God's design to make the spouse and the children holy is already at work. Peter directs the Christian wives to take advantage of their opportunity to win over the husband by their holy conduct (1 Pt 3:1). Christian spouses are meant to be a source of holiness for each other and, together, for their children.

Those saints too, who have followed their special vocation for a hidden life, a life of contemplation and prayer, have been a wonderful blessing for the whole world. The Carmelite Teresa of Avila is rightly honoured as "Doctor of the Church", and the Carmelite Thérèse of the Infant Jesus is honoured as patroness of the missions. Their whole life was filled with a burning zeal for the salvation of all people. Their writings as well as their biographies have inspired many along the road to holiness. We can say that where there is not a sense of mission, there is no real holiness yet.

Holy families are the most competent schools of holiness. Each member will make his or her contribution by fulfilling the respective role. They will acquire the necessary competence for it by mutual encouragement and common striving for discernment. The various Christian family movements bring together a great wealth of capacities, gifts and charisms. There, families learn together how to be holy and how to fulfil their mission for church and world.

Holy persons and communities are a living gospel by their very being. But they will also be watchful for the many opportunities to spell out the gospel and its implications for the ordering of life.

Holiness is not a garment to be hung up at the entrance to one's business or professional sphere; it is a vital part of oneself which affects the economic, cultural, social and political environment in which we move. It is creative first for healthy human relationships but also for healthier structures in all these realms. It implies outstanding honesty in fulfilling professional duties and in all public activities. Holy people, by their unselfish co-operation, bring a healthy atmosphere to their working milieu. They are constantly alert to improve human conditions in the realms of work and leisure.

Holiness surely does not shrink from political responsibility, since the welfare, security, peace and justice in the world depend upon political decisions. Hence the response to our calling to holiness requires also a serious preparation for fulfilling our role as citizens in and of the cultural and economic world.

Although holiness is a quality of persons and communities, it obliges people to fight urgently against all forms of collective egotism. Just as the sins of the many somehow grow together in the "sin of the world", so and much more should holy people and communities bring together all their forces to heal public life whenever and wherever it can be done.

It would be a grave error with disastrous consequences if holy people would shy away from such arduous vocations as politics, art, journalism, entertainment and the like. In all professions, but above all in those which most influence the lives and thinking of many, we need the witness and the talents of competent holy people.

In all these efforts to fulfil our mission we shall be watchful of our motives. We have to withstand all temptations to self-importance or self-glorification. The Lord warns us: "When you do some act of charity, do not announce it with a flourish of trumpets, as the hypocrites do in synagogue and in the streets to win admiration from men" (Mt 6:2). But when Jesus says, "your good deed must be secret, and your heavenly Father who sees what is done in secret will reward you" (Mt 6:4), we should not imagine that he means privatising sanctity. What he requests is absolute purity of motive: the desire to please God and to be unselfish in our relationships with others. We should not do good just for earthly reward. This is, indeed, also the condition to fulfil our mission to be "light for the world". We are not a shining light by ourselves but only through the one who can truthfully say, "I am the light of the world". Therefore we have to be constantly aware that the savour of life and the warmth of light are God's gifts, to be honoured as such by unselfish motives and generous use of the gifts.

* * *

Out of nothingness, O Lord, you have called me into being; out of darkness and sin you have called me to holiness. Here I am! Show me the way, day by day. Open my heart and mind for the surpassing knowledge of Christ, the Redeemer of the world. Lord, here I am; send me! Let me and all believers understand our mission to be light to the world, salt to the earth, yeast in the dough.

Forgive me, Father, for the many times I have endangered and dimmed the light that I could have been in your design. I have not sought enough the light of Christ. All too often I have been distracted and superficial and have missed the mark by aiming more at mere correctness than at holiness. Forgive me for trying so often to make myself the centre of life, while knowing quite well that we are truly alive only if we give all honour to you, the source of life and holiness.

Yet all my failures cannot rob me of my firm faith that you still call me to holiness. Therefore, let your light shine upon me and upon us all. Show us your gracious countenance and grant us your gifts of wisdom and discernment. Give us a grateful memory and fill our hearts, minds and wills with the energies of hope and trust. Transform us by the power of your holy love, so that our love may be ever more a mirror image of yours, thus to lead other people closer to you.

Lord, increase in all of us the faith in our vocation to holiness, and strengthen our sense of mission, to the glory of your name.